CUNARD
a photographic history

KINGSTOWN.
054. ST VINCENT

CUNARD
a photographic history

JANETTE McCUTCHEON

To QE2:
Whenever I have felt 'at sea', QE2 – my inspiration – has always
been there for me.

Thank you to my two favourite Cunarders – *Queen Mary* and
QE2 – and to the employees of Cunard for making the line the
greatest in the world

First published 2004

Tempus Publishing Ltd
The Mill, Brimscombe Port
Stroud, Gloucestershire GL5 2QG
www.tempus-publishing.com

British Library Cataloguing in Publication Data.
A catalogue record for this book is available from the British Library.

ISBN 0 7524 3001 7

Typesetting and origination by Tempus Publishing.
Printed and bound in Great Britain.

Contents

Preface

One-hundred-and-sixty-five years ago, a Nova Scotian entrepreneur called Samuel Cunard ventured across the Atlantic and founded the greatest shipping line the world has ever known. Still going strong today, the line he founded has had its ups and downs but it still retains the name of its founder, Cunard, and the orange-red and black funnels of his very first steamship. Its ships are amongst the most famous in the world, and there are few people alive who have not heard of at least one Cunarder, whether it is the *Lusitania*, the *Queen Mary*, *Queen Elizabeth 2* or its newest ship, *Queen Mary 2*.

I hope that within the 96 pages of this book you find some fascinating images which tell the story of this great British institution and its 165 years of heritage and history, something no other shipping line in the world can match. It has been fun collecting together so many previously unpublished views of the ships of Cunard and it was as difficult to decide what to drop from the selection of over 2,000 images I started with as it was to decide what should be in the book. For my favourite ships (the Queens) I had so much choice while for other vessels, especially the early ships, I found it difficult to find a representative selection. What has been good was to remind myself of just how many ships the company has owned and just how much a part the Cunard Line has played in the forging of three nations. Countless millions of people in America and Canada can lay claim to a descendant that travelled Cunard, countless lives have been saved in many wars as a result of the ships' abilities to carry huge numbers of soldiers in times of need and the ships themselves have been a part of maritime history from that first tiny ship that sailed from Liverpool in 1840 to today's largest passenger ship, *Queen Mary 2*. Cunard is a great institution, and one that deserves another 165 years of interesting history.

Acknowledgements

Like all books, this one would not have been possible without the help of numerous other people who have helped with information and support while the book was taking shape. Thanks are due to Jackie Webb at Wotton Lawn Library, Gloucester, for use of the library and the peace and solitude this provided while I was working on the text, Emma Jackson at Tempus Publishing for her help and suggestions with the design and my husband, Campbell, who has encouraged me to write this book.

Chapter One

Cunard's Conquest
of the Atlantic

Previous page: The first Cunard Royal Mail Ship, *Britannia*, leaving Liverpool on her maiden voyage to Halifax and Boston. The United States flag flies from her forward mast with the Red Ensign from her stern. Captain Henry Woodruff waves from the bridge, above the paddle wheels.

Left: Britannia lasted in Cunard service until 1849, when she was sold to the North German Confederate Navy and converted into a corvette called *Barbarossa*. In 1880 she was broken up after a long and fruitful life.

Safety first… followed by excellent service; those were the cornerstones of Samuel Cunard's philosophy for his newest and greatest venture. The Nova Scotian had decided to set up a transatlantic shipping company, carrying the mail and passengers from Liverpool to Halifax and Boston. It was at a time when steamships were only just beginning to pave their way across the Atlantic. For three or four decades they had steamed up rivers and across lakes but there had only been a few serious attempts to sail the Atlantic, culminating in Isambard Kingdom Brunel's *Great Western* and the *Sirius* of the British & American Steam Navigation Co. reaching New York within a few hours of each other in late April 1838. Cunard's aim was that passengers should arrive at their destination as safely as possible on a regular service. The cabins and creature comforts on Cunard's ships may not have been palatial, but at least there was a well-trained captain and crew who knew the ship and who wouldn't take risks with passengers' lives.

Samuel Cunard was the son of a master carpenter and timber merchant and was born in Halifax, Nova Scotia, in 1787. He showed entrepreneurial spirit at the age of seventeen when he managed his own general store. Later he joined his father in business and started exploring alternative money-making ventures, such as iron, shipping and coal.

A. Cunard & Son was set up by Abraham and Samuel Cunard and they became agents for the loading of ships to the West Indies and London, and one of the most efficient companies for loading and unloading cargo in Canada. Soon the Cunards had their own ships and they were carrying mail between Newfoundland, Boston and the British colony of Bermuda. At one point, Cunard had fifty sailing ships in service.

With his knowledge of shipping and the new steam technology, Samuel had the idea of the 'ocean railway', where passengers and cargo would arrive across the ocean at specific times on a timetabled service. This idea was greeted with disdain by some used to sail and the irregular sailings of most sailing vessels. Luckily, Cunard had the foresight and money to invest in the idea, and became one of the principal shareholders of the *Royal William*, the first ship to cross the Atlantic Ocean primarily by steam.

The *Royal William* was a positive experience for Samuel Cunard and in 1839 he submitted a bid to the British Government to establish a regular steamship service for mail from Liverpool to Halifax, Quebec and Boston. Cunard was the only ship-owner who would undertake crossing the Atlantic in winter as well as summer and to guarantee regular sailings, whatever the weather or numbers of passengers booked. Many ship-owners were discouraged by the winter trade as the Atlantic could be very treacherous for a small ship and many still disappeared without trace.

While finalising the mail contract in Britain, Cunard had to raise the necessary finance to build his ships. A mutual friend, James Melville of the East India Company, introduced him to the engineer Robert Napier, whose shipyard at Greenock on the Clyde agreed to design Cunard's first three 920-ton steam packets for £32,000 each.

On 4 May 1839, the formal mail contract was signed, but a dark cloud soon hung over the contract. Napier realised that the ships he had quoted

Above: To ensure fresh supplies of milk, meat and eggs, livestock was carried aboard the early steamers. Here, a cow is being herded aboard *Britannia*. This piece of artwork dates from the 1930s and was used in a Cunard brochure of the time.

Right: RMS *Britannia* had three near identical sister ships, all built in Greenock or Port Glasgow, Scotland. Here, *Britannia* is compared in size with the *Aquitania* of 1914.

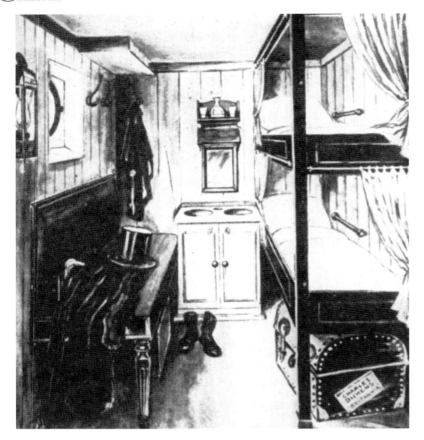

for would be too small to cope with the Atlantic. Instead, the ships would need to be at least 1,100 tons. Most of the finance for the new venture was raised in Scotland, with some coming from Liverpool ship-owners. Samual Cunard, George Burns, David McIver and eighteen other Glasgow businessmen shared in the partnership of the new vessels. The British & North American Royal Mail Steam Packet Company was formed and contracts placed with Clyde shipbuilders for the first four Cunard ocean liners. On 4 July, the same year, a revised agreement was signed between the British Government and Cunard.

It is often thought by most that the first Cunarder to sail the Atlantic was the *Britannia*, but a small feeder vessel called *Unicorn*, chartered from G.&J. Burns, sailed from Liverpool on 15 May 1840, arriving at Halifax with twenty-seven passengers on 1 June 1840. She was then used on the Halifax–Pictou–Quebec service.

On 4 July 1840, the Royal Mail Ship *Britannia*, the first of the four new vessels, sailed from Liverpool to Halifax, then on to Boston. In

Above left: One of the most famous of the early passengers was Charles Dickens, who travelled in *Britannia* in January 1842. He said of the ship that his cabin was an 'utterly impracticable, thoroughly hopeless and profoundly preposterous box'. The saloon was described as a 'long, narrow apartment, not unlike a gigantic hearse, with windows in the side'.

Above right: Built in 1843, *Hibernia* was the sixth Cunarder. Built by Robert Steele & Sons in Greenock, she was 240ft long and carried 215 passengers, 90 crew and 300 tons of cargo. She was sold in 1850 and became a Spanish naval ship, *Habanois*.

Right: An early poster from her first year of service advertising *Hibernia.*

Far right: One of the earliest known Cunard menus is this one from 17 October 1843. A far cry from today's fare on *Queen Mary 2.* I'm not sure that calves' heads would go down well today.

Below: Cambria, known as the 'Flying Cambria' was built in 1845.

HALIFAX AND BOSTON
ROYAL MAIL.

THE **HIBERNIA** starts on **WEDNESDAY**, the 4th of October. — *At Three o'Clock,* on the **Afternoon** of that day, a Steamer will be at the Egremont Slip, south end of the Prince's Dock, to take off the Passengers.

☞ Passengers are particularly requested to send all Luggage on board the day before.

BILL OF FARE.

STEAM SHIP HIBERNIA.

day of

BREAKFAST.

Dishes of Beef Steaks.
Do.   Mutton Chops.
Do.   Pork Chops.
Do.   Veal Cutlets.
Do.   Smoked Salmon.
Do.   Broiled Chicken.
Do.   Fried Ham.
Do.   Cold Meats.
Do.   Stews.
Eggs in Omelettes.
Do.   Boiled.
Hominy.
Mush.

DINNER.

	ROAST.	BOILED.
Soups		
Dishes Fish		
2 Do. Beef		
2 Do. Mutton		
Do. Lamb		
Do. Veal		
Do. Pork		
Do. Pigs		
Do. Turkeys		
Do. Geese		
Do. Ducks		
Do. Fowls		
Do. Curds		
Do. Stews		
Fricasee		
Made Dishes		
Calves' Heads		

VEGETABLES, ASSORTED.

PASTRY.

Apple Pies.
Do.   Puddings.
Raspberry Tarts.
Strawberry do.
Cranberry do.
Plum do.
Damson do.
Gooseberry do.
Roll Puddings.
Plum do.
Rice do.
Pancakes.
Omelettes.

W M Thackeray

T.J BOND

Thackeray, another early patron, returns from the United States in the "Europa."

addition to the transatlantic mail, she also carried sixty-three passengers. On this new ship, safety was paramount. The décor of the new paddle-steamer was not the most extravagant, but Cunard insisted that the new ship be built to the highest safety standards possible. The best and most trustworthy crew was employed – Cunard's reputation and the mail subsidy depended on it. What use were fancy cabins if the ship sank half way across the Atlantic?

Exactly one month later, on 4 August 1840, the second Cunard steam packet, *Arcadia*, set off from Liverpool for North America, followed by a third, *Caledonia*, in September. A few months later *Columbia* completed the foursome.

In August 1841, Cunard – encouraged by the Canadian Government – renegotiated the terms of the agreement with the British Government because the winter sailings were much more hazardous than expected. The company would receive £81,000 per annum for carrying the mails and a new fifth vessel was to be built as a reserve. On 19 April 1843, *Hibernia* came into service.

A few months later, *Columbia* grounded between Halifax and Boston. Although all eighty-five passengers were saved, the ship herself was a total loss. As a replacement, *Cambria* entered service in January 1845.

The battle of the mails began when the United States Government backed the formation of the Ocean Steam Navigation Co. (OSNC) to take the US mails from New York to Southampton, then on to Bremen. Because of this threat, Cunard renegotiated the British contract for the American mails and established a weekly mail service to New York in summer and a fortnightly service in winter. The 1,422-ton *Hibernia* inaugurated the Liverpool–New York service.

Left above: Another famous passenger was William Makepeace Thackeray, who returned from the United States aboard *Europa*, Cunard's eleventh ship. *Europa* continued the tradition of Clyde-built Cunarders and was constructed in Port Glasgow. She was involved in a tragic accident on her second voyage when she collided with and sank the barque *Charles Bartlett* with the loss of 115 lives.

Left: The first ship for the new Mediterranean service was *Balbec*, built by William Denny at Dumbarton. Used initially on the service from Liverpool to Constantinople, she was also run on the Liverpool–New York and Liverpool–Le Havre routes. She was wrecked off Land's End in March 1884.

In February 1844, it looked like the RMS *Britannia* was going to be trapped by ice at Boston. The residents, realising just how important the mail ship was to their city, cut a four-mile route through the ice so that the *Britannia* could sail with the mails to England.

To compete with the Ocean Steam Navigation Co., four new British & North American Steam Packet Co. ships took to the Atlantic in 1848 – *America*, *Niagara*, *Europa* and *Canada*. These would be faster than their American counterparts. The battle for the fastest crossing of the Atlantic had begun.

In 1850 a new American line appeared – the Collins Line – owned by Edward Collins. The US Government subsidised the line, and Collins' four new ships soon appeared from New York shipyards. *Atlantic*, *Pacific*, *Arctic* and *Baltic* were bigger and fancier than the Cunarders and could match Cunard's regular steam packet service to America. They were the official United States Mail Ships and, as such, were subsidised in the way that the Cunarders were.

The passenger market had become increasingly competitive too. It was a way the steamship companies

*Queen Victoria bidding farewell
to troops proceeding to Russia.*

*First iron Cunarder
under construction.*

Top: Queen Victoria waving troops off as they went to the Crimea to fight against the Russians.

Left: The first iron-hulled passenger liner on the Atlantic was *Persia*, built in 1856 and the longest vessel afloat at 376ft when built.

Above: This aquatint engraving shows *Persia* at sea. She was commanded for most of her career by Captain Lott who sailed in her over 300 times. She struck an iceberg on her maiden voyage but arrived safely at her destination, while the Collins Line ship *Pacific*, which had left Liverpool the day before, sank without trace in the mid-Atlantic.

could easily increase their profits, as well as carrying the mail. Many of the passengers had business interests in both the US and Europe, and a reliable passenger service was needed. These business passengers tended to choose the fastest ships because, to them, time was indeed money. At a time when crossing the Atlantic was measured in weeks, a few days saved could make a huge difference to business. It helped if the ships were nicely decorated too, as the fare-paying passengers preferred not to be reminded that they were in the middle of the ocean, but rather in some grand country house.

Competition increased for the fastest and grandest ships afloat. Cunard's accommodation was very basic in comparison with some other lines, but for other companies, safety just wasn't a priority. Cunard ordered two more ships – *Arabia* and *Persia* – to compete with the Collins Line in terms of creature comforts for passengers.

The Collins Line's main aim was luxury for the passenger and a speedy trip across the Atlantic. The ships provided restaurant-quality food and the best accommodation afloat, and this took business away from Cunard's vessels. But, for Collins, 1854 was a terrible year. The Collins liner *Arctic* collided in dense fog with a French

H.R.H. Prince Alfred, the Sailor Prince, returns home from Canada by the "Arabia."

Above: Prince Alfred, the Sailor Prince, travelled in the *Arabia* from Boston in 1861.

Right: The *Scotia* and a later Cunard flyer, the *Mauretania* of 1907. *Scotia* was the last of the Cunard paddle steamers before the line converted to screw propellers. She held the Blue Riband for five years from 1863–1869 with an average speed of 14.02 knots.

The "Scotia" and the "Mauretania."

steamer and all in all 322 souls were lost, including Edward Collins' wife and daughter. This, together with the loss of the *Pacific* in 1856, and high running and labour costs, forced the Collins Line into bankruptcy later that year.

As the passenger trade across the Atlantic increased, Cunard decided to venture into other areas. The first Mediterranean cargo service started in 1853 with the ships *Taurus*, *Melita*, *Jura* and *Balbec*.

When the Crimean War started in 1854, Cunard faced huge problems when the Admiralty requisitioned and operated eleven of their vessels as troopships and hospital ships. Their North Atlantic trade all but disappeared as ships were requisitioned for use in the conflict. As the war ended, Cunard then started to think about returning their remaining vessels to the North Atlantic trade. In addition to the existing fleet, the first new ship to be built was *Persia*, Cunard's first iron-hulled ship. She was the longest ship afloat at the time. The *Persia* sailed for New York the day after the Collins Line *Pacific*. Even after scraping an iceberg on her maiden voyage, the *Persia* arrived safely in New York. Unfortunately, the *Pacific* was never heard from again. Both had been trying to gain the Blue Riband.

The Blue Riband was the pennant given to the fastest crossing of the Atlantic from Bishop's Rock, off the Scilly Isles, to Ambrose Light in the United States. Many ships tried to achieve this on their maiden voyage, as the publicity would ensure that passengers would want to travel in that particular ship or its sister vessels. For first-class passengers, it meant that they would arrive faster at their destination, and for the steerage passengers it would be something to boast about to their friends and relatives.

A whole new market opened up for passenger lines in the 1860s – emigrants. As America became the land of opportunity and more and more of the country was being opened up, the shipping lines were helping to sustain a much more regular flow of people from Europe

Top: Calabria, named in 1870, was originally called *Australasian*. Although built in 1857, she was sold to Cunard in 1859. In 1876 she became a cable ship and was scrapped in Holland in 1897.

Middle: One of the earliest known photographs of a Cunard liner is this one of *Hecla*, from 1860. Although of very poor quality, it shows the stern of the ship. She was designed for the Mediterranean service and as a relief ship for the transatlantic route. She lasted in one guise or another until 1954 when she was scrapped after being used for many years as a floating pontoon.

Bottom: RMS *China* made her maiden voyage in March 1862 to New York, on a sailing that connected with the *British Queen* for Nassau, Bahamas.

to the United States and Canada. People were needed in North America to sustain businesses and help to construct and maintain the expanding infrastructure. The United States began welcoming people who were healthy and willing enough to work and seek their fortune. Opportunities were endless and whole families emigrated from Europe to America on board the liners. Men would go to America, make enough money, and pay for their wives and families to come across at a later date. The entire continent was becoming a vast melting pot for men and women of all races who all desired a new life away from political, social and economic conditions at home.

At the same time, other countries, notably France and Germany, were starting up their own shipping companies to compete for the emigrant traffic, and the Atlantic was becoming a busy place. Cunard was building larger and faster ships to compete against the new entrants to the trade and, as a result, *China* and *Scotia* were put on the North Atlantic service in 1862.

America's Civil War started in 1863 and everything changed for the shipping lines. The emigrant traffic basically stopped and people ceased travelling between Europe and America. The only saving grace was that both sides now needed war supplies, and most of Cunard's ships could take cargo. During the war, Sir Samuel Cunard died peacefully at his home in London on 28 April 1865.

After the Civil War ended, there was again a flood of emigrants to the United States. Jobs needed to be filled, businesses needed staff,

Opposite above: British Queen was owned by Burns & MacIver but was used on the Nassau run in conjunction with the transatlantic sailings. She was purchased by Cunard in 1878. After forty-nine years' service she was sold for scrap in 1898.

Opposite below: Two views of *Marathon,* built for the Mediterranean service. She was modernised and lengthened in 1873 and was used as a troopship in the Egyptian campaign of 1882. In 1898 she was sold to Workman, Clark in Belfast, in part payment for *Cypria.*

This page, above and below: Wrecked off Cape Cornwall in October 1889, RMS *Malta* was constructed in 1865. Designed mainly for third-class and steerage passengers, she carried 593 Steerage and forty-six cabin passengers. All of the passengers and crew were rescued from the ship when she foundered.

farms needed farmers and cattle hands, and railroads needed employees. Opportunities were endless. For the oppressed and poor of Western Europe, America was an attainable dream, and companies like Cunard, the means of achieving them.

As Cunard ordered new ships to compete on the North Atlantic route, *Samaria*, *Abyssinia* and *Algeria* entered service between 1868 and 1871.

Until 1871, Cunard had had supremacy on the North Atlantic highway, but this was all about to change. A bright, new shining star was about to burst onto the scene. The new White Star Line, owned by Thomas Ismay, took shipboard luxury to a new dimension. His brand new ships, *Oceanic*, *Atlantic*, *Baltic* and *Republic*, were designed to be the most modern ships afloat with every modern design feature and innovation. The White Star Line had led everyone to believe they were building for the Australian trade, so it was a bit of a shock to discover

four brand new liners on the North Atlantic. Luxury abounded and the ingenious devices on board included lamps rather than candles, bathtubs and central heating. Many houses did not even have these luxuries yet! Passengers flocked to the new White Star ships and other lines started to see a dip in their trade. Cunard's entire fleet had just become obsolete overnight and bigger and better ships had to be designed just to compete with the new levels of standard and luxury that the White Star Line had introduced.

Above: RMS *Russia* was built by J.&G. Thompson of Clydebank (the forerunner of John Brown's) in 1867 and was the last Cunarder built with a clipper stern. She was sold in 1881 to the Red Star Line and renamed *Waesland*. In 1902 she was sunk off Holyhead, Anglesey, after a collision with the Houston Line *Harmonides*.

Chapter Two

From the 'First Modern Liner' to the End of the First World War

Previous page: Umbria casting off from the quayside at Liverpool, *c.*1890.

Above: Bothnia, under full sail. She made her maiden voyage on 8 August 1874 from Liverpool to New York. In 1899 she was broken up in Italy.

Below: Scythia at Liverpool – she was the second of the *Bothnia*-class ships and also lasted to be broken up in 1899 in Italy.

Opposite: The *Gallia*, regarded as the parent of the modern liner, was built in 1879 and was a vast improvement in terms of luxury and design over her two older sisters. She survived barely a year after *Bothnia* and *Scythia*, having been wrecked on her maiden voyage for the Allan line in 1900.

The "Gallia," regarded as the parent of modern liners.

As competition grew for the biggest, fastest and grandest ships on the Atlantic, and the new White Star Line became more of a threat, Cunard had to compete. Their answer was *Bothnia*, built in 1874, and the first of the Cunarders to just about be able to compete on luxury terms with the new builds from White Star, although still falling short of the luxury of the White Star ships. She and her sisters, RMS *Gallia* and *Scythia*, were the finest ships built in the 1870s for Cunard. The *Gallia*, last of the trio, was described in a Cunard publication as 'designed to beat all competitors, and to go one better in regard to her internal fittings'. The result was that passengers flocked to sail in her. Although still fitted with auxiliary sails, she was really the mother of all modern liner development.

Cunard built their first steel-hulled passenger ship, RMS *Servia*, in 1881. She could travel at 17 knots. After her came the *Aurania*, but she

was not as successful as her owners had hoped. On her maiden voyage, her engines overheated and she had to complete the journey under sail. Her beam was also so narrow that she had a tendency to roll. She and *Servia* were both requisitioned for Boer War troop transport duties.

During 1884, Cunard Line took over the Guion liner, *Oregon*. The new luxury liner promptly won Cunard the coveted Blue Riband. After that, Cunard then decided to compete seriously with the White Star Line's new vessels and built *Etruria* and *Umbria*. The excellent safety record (not a life lost in passenger trade since the company was started) was now being complemented by their ultra-modern new liners and second-to-none service.

Another challenger to Cunard's success came in the form of the Inman Line. Their ships, *City of Paris* and *City of New York*, were a great

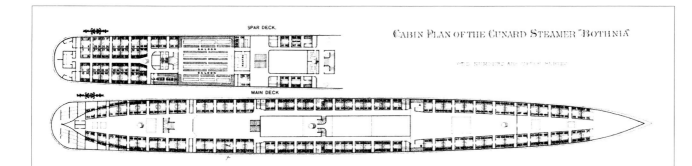

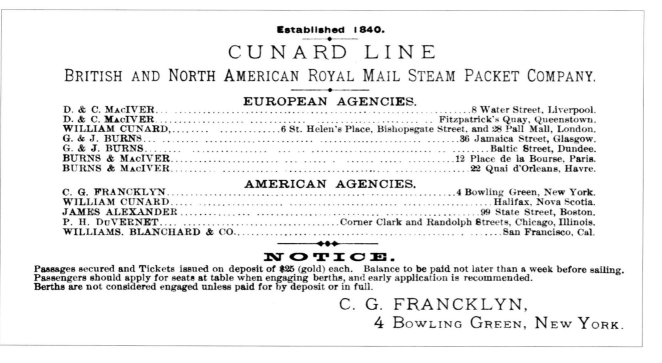

Above: The deck plan of *Bothnia*, from 1874.

Below: It is interesting to see that the Cunard Line (as it became known in 1878) was still using agencies founded by the original investors in the 1840 company.

success and with their clipper bows and triple funnels were very pretty too. White Star challenged these vessels by building *Teutonic* and *Majestic*. Soon after, in 1893, Cunard commissioned *Campania* and *Lucania*. These two Clyde-built liners again took Cunard to new heights of luxury and speed. *Campania* took the Blue Riband on only her second voyage and *Lucania* promptly won it from *Campania* on her maiden voyage. *Lucania* was the first Cunarder to publish a daily newspaper for her passengers, this being collated from news messages received by the new-fangled wireless.

Kaiser Wilhelm der Grosse was the first new ship to pose any major threat to the two Cunarders. Built by the German company Norddeutscher Lloyd, she went into service in 1897. The *Kaiser* was an extremely beautiful and elegant ship and was the first four-funnelled liner. She was also the fastest and most luxurious transatlantic liner of her day.

In 1903 Cunard purchased the *Pannonia* and *Slavonia* on the stocks for their new emigrant Fiume–Gibraltar–New York route, as the company had agreed a ten-year contract with the Hungarian

Above: Two years after *Gallia* came *Catalonia*, which was broken up in 1901 by Thomas Ward, after being purchased for scrap for £10,305.

Below: Servia, when built in 1881, was the second largest ship afloat, after Brunel's *Great Eastern.*

Government to move emigrants to the United States, starting in 1904. *Ultonia*, of 1898, and *Carpathia*, of 1904, were also used on the service. *Ultonia*'s maiden voyage was on the Liverpool–Boston service as a cattle and cargo carrier but she was transferred to the Hungarian emigrant service in 1904, with little conversion work to turn her into a passenger ship. The other ship, *Carpathia*, was to become famous in 1912 as the rescue ship for *Titanic* survivors. In 1914, she also had the dubious honour of carrying Gavrilo Princip and the other assassins to Sarajevo to kill Archduke Franz Ferdinand, an event that started the First World War.

Cunard ships took many emigrants to the United States. The ships would offload third-class passengers for inspection and forward travel at Ellis Island. The inspection was very important as anyone with any serious health problems would be sent back on the next Cunard ship at the company's expense. Many companies routinely inspected the passengers before they travelled up the

Royal Artillery embarking in Liverpool for Zulu War.

The "Aurania"—Ola and New.

Top: Cunard ships were again called upon to go to war when the Zulu War of 1879 erupted. Here the Royal Artillery leave Liverpool for Southern Africa.

Left: A view of the *Aurania* of 1883 and her namesake of 1924.

Above: An 1879s Cunarder.

Above: A period trade card, from 1874, used to advertise the new luxury service offered by the RMS *Bothnia.*

Below: A view of the *Bothnia* taken from an 1870s trade card issued to prospective passengers.

Clockwise from top left:
Never a popular ship as her narrow beam caused her to roll a lot, *Aurania* is shown here in her guise as a Boer War troop transport in South African waters.

RMS *Aurania* at Liverpool in the 1890s.

The Guion liner *Oregon*, purchased in June 1884, became a Blue Riband holder for Cunard. She sank after colliding with an unknown wooden schooner (probably the *Charles Morse*, which disappeared at the same time). All 641 passengers and 241 crew were rescued along with 600 bags of mail.

Cephalonia was built in dry dock at Liverpool, the largest ship constructed on the Mersey at the time. She ended her life at Port Arthur and was sunk as a blockship in 1904 during the Russo-Japanese War.

gangplank to board the ship to check their health was in order and to save money on emigrants being returned.

Although the first- and second-class passengers had most of the space on board these liners, it was the emigrant classes that kept the shipping lines in business. The emigrants had to put up with very cramped conditions with none of the luxuries of the more superior classes of accommodation. In those days it was just accepted that this was the way it was. The emigrants had to share four, or possibly even six, to a cramped, tiny cabin. In the elegant suites above them, there would possibly be one person or a couple with a maid or manservant in a suite of four rooms. The food was also of a totally different standard. Even the accommodation was totally different. First- and second-classes had

Clockwise from top left:
Built by John Elder at Govan, Cunard's *Etruria* and *Umbria* set new standards again for transatlantic passenger ships. The last Cunarders to have auxiliary sails, here *Etruria* is shown under sail.

Umbria or *Etruria* at Liverpool's landing stage at the turn of the twentieth century. *Umbria* was used as a Boer War transport and in 1903 an attempt was made to blow her up in New York with a case of dynamite. She was broken up in 1910.

Silhouetted as she lies on the Mersey at the Cunard buoy, *Etruria* is passed by a sailing ship. She was fitted for wireless in 1901 (one of the first ships to be so fitted) and in 1909 she was sold for breaking at Preston.

ornate wood panelling and mouldings, beautiful chandeliers, and the most luxurious of furniture. In third-class the walls were the metal skin of the ship, complete with rivets, and the furniture was composed of basic metal seats, benches and tables.

At the turn of the twentieth century, Cunard built another two vessels to join *Ultonia* on the Liverpool–Boston cargo/passenger route – *Ivernia* and *Saxonia*.

In 1902, a new threat came from America. John Pierpoint Morgan, a financier, started buying up shipping companies, with his International Navigation Co. as holding company, in an attempt to create a monopoly on the North Atlantic route and use this to fix prices at a fair and reasonable level. Amongst his takeovers were the Dominion Line,

American Line, Leyland Line and Red Star Line. The most worrying of all was the purchase of the White Star Line. Cunard felt they were next in line for a hostile takeover and fought off the competition. But Cunard's main fear was that this new company, renamed the International Mercantile Marine (IMM), would run them out of business. In the beginning IMM was not profitable, but along with the German lines, they were soon causing Cunard problems on the North Atlantic route as their ships began to take the cream of the passenger trade.

From the British Government's viewpoint, the White Star takeover was worrying. Cunard and White Star were the predominant British transatlantic lines. If both these major British lines were taken over by an American company, then this would ultimately reduce the British

Left: Campania, with *Lucania* in the distance, about to leave from Liverpool's Landing Stage, *c.*1894. By April 1914 she had made 250 return voyages to New York, and was sold for scrapping later that year. She did, however, have a new lease of life as she was sold to the Admiralty for conversion to a seaplane carrier.

Below: A passenger list from 1896.

Opposite, above and middle: There were no new Cunarders for almost ten years, and then came *Campania* and *Lucania*, two new flyers. Each ship could carry 2,000 passengers and 400 crew. *Campania*, on her second voyage, captured the Blue Riband, while *Lucania* took the Blue Riband from her in October 1893. Through 1894, the ships swapped the award with *Lucania* proving marginally faster at 21.75 knots in October of that year. Here, both ships are shown on their sea trials at Greenock, Scotland.

Opposite below: From 1895 Cunard began construction of a series of cargo ships. Here is a receipt from Workman, Clark of Belfast for part payment of their yard no.142, SS *Cypria*.

Cunard Line

Second Cabin

Passenger List

LIVERPOOL

to NEW YORK & BOSTON

VIA QUEENSTOWN.

PRINCIPAL AGENCIES

NEW YORK - 29. BROADWAY.   MANCHESTER - 98. MOSLEY STREET.
BOSTON - 126. STATE STREET.   GLASGOW - 30. JAMAICA STREET.
CHICAGO - 67. DEARBORN ST.   LEITH - - EXCHANGE BUILDINGS
LONDON - 32. COCKSPUR ST. S.W.   QUEENSTOWN - CUNARD WHARF
          93. BISHOPSGATE ST. E.C.   PARIS - - - 2 BIS. RUE SCRIBE

Head Offices. 8. Water St. & I. Rumford St..

LIVERPOOL.

Government's troop-carrying capacity in the event of war. After negotiations between the British Government and IMM, it was agreed that the White Star Line should still sail under the British flag, with British officers and crew. As the new International Mercantile Marine Co. was trying to buy Cunard as well, the British Government agreed that it would award Cunard a subsidy. This would ensure that Cunard remained independent. A condition of this subsidy was that Cunard could not be bought by IMM or any other foreign interest. The underlying reason was that if Cunard remained loyal to the British flag, then Cunard ships could be requisitioned in the event of war. The Government arranged a part-subsidy, part-loan for two new liners, which would be able to maintain a minimum speed of 24.5 knots in moderate weather. The ships also had to be designed to be converted into Armed Merchant Cruisers in the event of war. Cunard therefore agreed to remain British and not to allow major foreign investment. The new liners were to be known as *Mauretania* and *Lusitania* and they were to join the exulted ranks of the most famous liners of all time.

1905 saw the introduction of the 'pretty sisters' on the North Atlantic route – the first *Caronia* and the first *Carmania*. The *Caronia* was the slower of the two ships, having been fitted with quadruple-expansion engines, while her sister *Carmania* was fitted with steam turbines. Cunard wanted to experiment to see if the new-fangled steam turbines were more effective and economical than quadruple-expansion compound engines. In order to do this, both ships were similarly designed, but one was fitted with steam turbines and one with quadruple-expansion compound engines. *Carmania*, with the steam turbines, was always the faster and more economical ship and paved the way for the new technology to be fitted to the new Cunarders, *Lusitania* and *Mauretania*.

Excitement was growing as shipbuilding companies vied to build Cunard's new 'monster ships'. After tendering, the contracts were awarded to John Brown & Co. in Clydebank (for the *Lusitania*) and Swan, Hunter & Wigham Richardson on the Tyne (for the *Mauretania*). The *Lusitania* was the first 'monster ship' and entered service on 7 September 1907, followed by the *Mauretania* in November 1907. In answer to these new superliners, the German Hamburg Amerika Line and the White Star Line commissioned their own 'monster ships'. White Star built the *Olympic* and *Titanic* side by side, and eventually followed with *Britannic*. Hamburg Amerika built *Imperator* and *Vaterland*, followed by *Bismarck*. Cunard added *Aquitania*, the 'World's Wonder Ship' in 1914 as a riposte to the third sisters from their competitors.

Lusitania proved her mettle and took the Blue Riband on her second voyage. She maintained an average speed of 24 knots on this and on most of her other runs across the Atlantic. *Mauretania* challenged and took the Blue Riband from her on her maiden voyage, beating *Lusitania*'s record by 21 minutes.

Cunard added their first dual-purpose ships to their fleet in 1911. *Franconia* and *Laconia* were fitted out with the ability to undertake the North Atlantic trade in summer and then go cruising in winter. Unfortunately, neither ship had a long life as they were both torpedoed during the First World War, *Franconia* in 1916, north east of Malta, and *Laconia* in February 1917 off Ireland.

During 1911 Cunard re-entered the Canadian trade with the purchase of Geo. Thompson's Canadian interests, including the ships *Ascania*, *Ausonia* and *Albania*. In 1912, Cunard took over the Anchor Line. In that same year, their ship *Carpathia* became famous when she rescued survivors from the ill-fated *Titanic*.

Above: Campania in the Mersey, 1912, from an original watercolour.

Middle and below: Two different views of *Campania* and *Lucania* showing their huge funnels. *Lucania* was burned out in Liverpool in 1909. She was sold for scrap, making 17 knots on the way to the breakers in Swansea.

Opposite page
Above left: Liverpool Landing Stage, showing just how busy it could be on sailing day.

Above right: Lucania at the Stage, with the paddle tug *Pathfinder* and, in the Mersey, the *Great Britain*.

Below: By 1900, Swan & Hunter had built *Ivernia* for Cunard. Her funnel was 106ft tall from the boat deck to the rim of the cowl.

Cunard Bulletin.

R.M.S. "LUCANIA," from New York to Liverpool Oct. 3rd, 1903.

MARCONIGRAMS.

☞ Signor Marconi on Board. Shore Communications all through voyage.

Sunday, Oct. 4th, 1903.

Position.
Lat. 40.51 N.   Long. 66.27 W.
Distance from Queenstown 2462 miles
    ,,   Sandy Hook Lship 513   ,,

Communication with Marconi Station at Babylon from 6 p.m. till 9 p.m. Saturday, October 3rd. Distance from ship to station 45 miles. Passengers Telegrams were duly exchanged.

Communication with Marconi Station at Sagaponack from 9.50 p.m. Saturday, Oct. 3, till 1 a.m Sunday 4th. Distance from ship to station 65 miles. Passengers telegrams were duly exchanged.

Communication with Marconi Station at Nantucket from 1 a.m till 6 a.m. Distance from ship to station 96 Miles. Service and passengers telegrams were duly exchanged.

Communication was established with the Marconi Station at Cape Cod from 7 till 7.30 a.m. Private Telegrams were received. Distance from ship to Station 80 miles.

Communication was established with the Marconi Station at Glace Bay (Canada) from 10.30 a.m till 11.30 a.m. Distance from Station to Ship 800 miles. Private Telegrams were received.

Communication was established with Glace Bay, (Canada) from 8 p.m till 9.00 p.m. Distance 350 miles.

Latest News Received from Glace Bay

New York, Oct. 4th, 1903.

Seven killed and five injured in the collapse of the Corning Distillery building, Peoria, Illinois.

CUNARD-ÅNGARE VID LANDNINGSPLATSEN I LIVERPOOL.
(SNABBASTE ATLANTERRESA 5⅓ DYGN)

The birth of the ocean newspaper.

Opposite page, clockwise from top left:
Another innovation for Cunard was the publication of a daily newspaper. This is the first ever *Cunard Bulletin* from October 1903, printed on board *Lucania*.

An advert postcard from the Swedish agent showing *Campania* at the Stage, Liverpool.

Older ships were still in use as the new, modern vessels came into service. This is *Etruria* at Liverpool, *c.*1904.

The printing presses on board *Lucania*, showing the birth of the ocean newspaper.

Above: Built for the Boston route, this view shows either *Ivernia* or *Saxonia* in mid-ocean. The cost of each ship was £400,000 and they could carry 1,956 passengers, 1,600 of whom were third-class, with 164 first-class and 202 second-class.

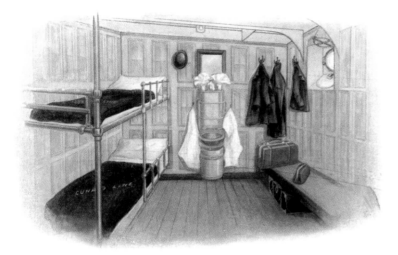

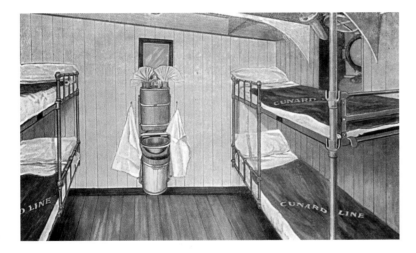

Opposite page
Top left: A third-class dinning room on a Cunard liner, *c*.1905.

Top right: In second-class, dining still involved being seated at benches, but in more pleasant surroundings with better food.

Middle left: A third-class smoking room.

Middle right: The second-class saloon was also not only more palatial, but much more comfortable, with upholstered seats and benches.

Bottom left: Third-class reading room.

Bottom right: Second-class reading room.

This page
Top left: A cabin for two people in third-class.

Top right: Here is a rather more luxurious second-class cabin for two people.

Above left: A cabin for four in third-class.

Above right: Third-class promenade deck.

S. S. „Saxonia" Landing Stage, Liverpool,

Above: Saxonia at Liverpool, *c.*1904.

Below: In 1905, Cunard built two new ships to test and compare the new turbine technology. *Carmania*, fitted with turbines, was almost identical to her sister, *Caronia*, fitted with reciprocating engines. The trials showed that not only was *Carmania* faster but the fuel consumption was better too.

Opposite: A sectional view through *Caronia*'s decks.

Far right: Caronia and *Carmania* at Quebec, after being placed on the Canadian run in 1923.

CUNARDER AT QUEENSTOWN

Above: Cooks aboard RMS *Caronia*.

Below: One of the most famous Cunarders is *Carpathia*, built for the new route from Hungary to America. She rescued all of the survivors from the *Titanic* disaster. *Pannonia*, *Ultonia* and *Slavonia* were also built for the Hungarian service. This view is of *Pannonia* at Fiume.

Above: *Carmania* at Queenstown. In 1913 she rescued two-thirds of the passengers from the Canadian Northern Line's SS *Volturno*, which burned out in the mid-Atlantic.

Below: *Caronia* at Madeira, while cruising *c*.1912.

„CUNARD"   MAGYAR-AMERIKAI VONAL.

VENICE

TRIESTE

R.M.S "SAXONIA" LEAVING FIUME.

Menu

Hors d'Œuvres

Créme Longchamps

Filets d'Aurora—Meuniére

Tournedos—Renaissance

Dindonneau Rôti—Farci
Salàde Romaine

Soufflé Rothschild

Dessert   Café

Above left: An Odin Rosenvinge poster advertising the Fiume service, showing *Saxonia*, used on the Mediterranean service in 1909 and 1912.

Above: Food, glorious food! A private dinner menu from *Caronia*, 1908.

Left: After the trials of *Caronia* and *Carmania*, it was decided to fit turbines to the two new express liners being designed and built at John Brown's, Clydebank, and Swan, Hunter & Wigham Richardson, Newcastle. Here, *Lusitania*, the first of the superliners, is shown in the fitting-out basin at Clydebank.

S.S. LUSITANIA.
IN GRAVING DOCK.

Left: Bow shots of the two fastest ships of the Edwardian period. On the left is *Lusitania* and on the right is *Mauretania*.

Below left: RMS *Mauretania* entering the dock system at Liverpool to be dry-docked after her sea trials off Eyemouth, Berwickshire, Scotland.

Below right: *Lusitania* compared with the New Brighton tower.

Opposite page
Above left: *Lusitania* (captioned as her sister *Mauritania* [*sic*]), outward bound, off Rock Ferry, Cheshire.

Middle left: In 1911, Cunard re-opened their Canadian service with the purchase of Geo. Thomson's Canadian ships.

Below left: New ships were built for the Canadian route, including the *Albania*, shown here off Cowes, Isle of Wight. She was sold after a year as she proved unsatisfactory for Cunard.

Right: On the morning of 15 April 1912, *Carpathia*, under the command of A.H. Rostron, sailed to the rescue of the survivors of the *Titanic* disaster. At tremendous risk, she sailed at almost 17 knots for four hours and picked up the 705 survivors from the lifeboats.

Comparison Picture to Scale
New Brighton Tower   621 ft high

R.M.S. Lusitania and Mauretania   790 ft long

R.M.S. Mauritania off Rock Ferry.

CUNARD LINE

"TITANIC" LIFEBOAT ALONGSIDE "CARPATHIA"

J. W. Barker, Copyright.

CUNARD LINER "AQUITANIA" AFLOAT

Above: The pre-war pinnacle of achievement for Cunard was the construction of *Aquitania*, built at John Brown's. Here she is seen immediately after her launch.

Below: Aquitania was the epitomy of the 'country house' ship, with interiors that would have not looked out of place in some Georgian 'pile'. Her swimming pool was utter luxury in comparison with what had gone before.

On 23 April 1913, the largest Cunarder then built, weighing in at 45,000 tons, was launched. *Aquitania*, as she was known, sailed on 31 May 1914 on her maiden voyage from Liverpool to New York. This was overshadowed by the recent loss of the *Empress of Ireland* with the loss of over 1,000 lives, when she collided with the collier *Storstadt* near Rimouski in the St Lawrence River in Canada. Six journeys and two months later and the world was at war. The *Aquitania*, along with her smaller sisters, *Lusitania* and *Mauretania*, was requisitioned for troop-carrying duties during the First World War. *Mauretania* and *Aquitania* survived the war, but *Lusitania* was sunk by the German U-boat U-20 in May 1915 while on a regular transatlantic sailing. Despite warnings in the American press, she sailed into sight of the U-20 off the Old Head of Kinsale as she slowed down on her trip into Queenstown (now Cobh), in County Cork. Within eighteen minutes, 1,198 lives were lost and the Americans brought to the brink of war with Germany.

By the end of the First World War, Cunard had lost twenty-two of its fleet, including *Lusitania*, *Carpathia*, *Franconia*, *Laconia* and *Folia*. The ships ranged from the second-largest ship of the fleet to lowly cargo vessels. In order to replace these losses and maintain a presence in the North Atlantic, Cunard ordered thirteen new ships in the immediate post-war period. This was the largest tonnage order ever placed by one company for ships.

As an extremely welcome addition to the Cunard fleet, the German liner *Imperator* was purchased by Cunard as war reparation for the loss of the *Lusitania*. Cunard renamed her *Berengaria* and converted her to oil burning. She was the largest ship in the fleet at over 52,000grt. She was in Cunard service until electrical problems caused her withdrawal from service in 1938. She had a propensity to roll, being a little bit top heavy but was known affectionately as Cunard's 'Happy Ship'.

Top: On Britain's largest liner, the restaurant was double height.

Bottom: Making her maiden voyage in May 1914, *Aquitania* was pulled off the Atlantic run in August after six voyages. She was a magnificent vessel, with even second-class having a palatial two-deck-high dining room.

Opposite page

Top left: Plunged headlong into war, Cunard lost many ships in the ensuing struggle, including *Lusitania* to a German torpedo off the Old Head of Kinsale, near Queenstown (now Cobh), Ireland, in May 1915.

Top right: Other losses included *Ivernia*, torpedoed on 1 January 1917, off Cape Matapan, Italy, while carrying 2,800 troops to Alexandria.

Middle left: Ausonia was sunk after being torpedoed off Fastnet Rock, Ireland, on 30 May 1918. Her crew and passengers were in the lifeboats for eight days before being rescued.

Middle right: It was not all bad news for the line, as *Carmania* sank the German Armed Merchant Cruiser *Cap Trafalgar* (which was disguised as *Carmania* at the time).

Bottom left: Phrygia, one of the cargo ships, sank a submarine in 1915. She survived the war and was scrapped in 1933.

Bottom right: Valeria, purchased in 1915, also destroyed a submarine by gunfire but was destroyed by fire in the Mersey in March 1918.

This page

Above: Volodia, her sister ship, was less lucky, being torpedoed on 21 August 1917 off Ushant, France.

Below: Two ships that gave distinguished service were *Mauretania* and *Aquitania*. Both were used as Armed Merchant Cruisers, hospital ships and troopships. Here, *Mauretania* shows off her dazzle-paint livery, designed by Norman Wilkinson to confuse German submarines.

Above: Aquitania, painted in dazzle paint, in New York after bringing back US Afro-American soldiers. One complete division, commanded by Maj. Gen. Chas. Ballou, fought in the Vosges mountains.

Below: Rammed on 5 November 1918 by HMS *Glorious*, *Campania* almost survived the conflict. Her funnels slipped below the waters of the Firth of Forth, just off Burntisland, a casualty of a tragic accident.

Above: Here *Aquitania* is shown as a hospital ship during the Gallipoli campaign.

Below: Although sold to the Admiralty, the *Campania* served too, as a seaplane carrier.

Above: A rather distant shot of AMC *Carmania* stopping the French Line ship, *France*, in International waters outside New York in September 1914.

Below: Of the Canadian ships, none of the trio of sisters, *Aulania, Ausonia* and *Andania* survived the war. This rare view shows one of them in wartime.

Top right: Carmania in her war paint.

Middle right: In 1914 the largest troop convoy ever assembled to date arrived at Plymouth from Canada. Here *Aulania,* or *Andania,* is seen in Plymouth Harbour with *Laurentic* and *Megantic* of the White Star Line.

Bottom right: In the spring of 1918, *Mauretania* brought 33,000 American soldiers to Europe.

Crew and soldiers abandoning ship, HMT *Ivernia*, in December 1916.

Above: It was never considered that *Aquitania*'s garden lounge should become a hospital ward.

Below: Or that her first-class lounge should be filled to bursting with hospital beds and patients.

Above: Aquitania entering
Southampton Water in 1917 and
passing a fleet of 'Q' ships – disguised
armed merchantmen.

Left: The price of war – graves at
Queenstown of the victims of the
Lusitania.

From the End of
the First World War
to the 'Queens'

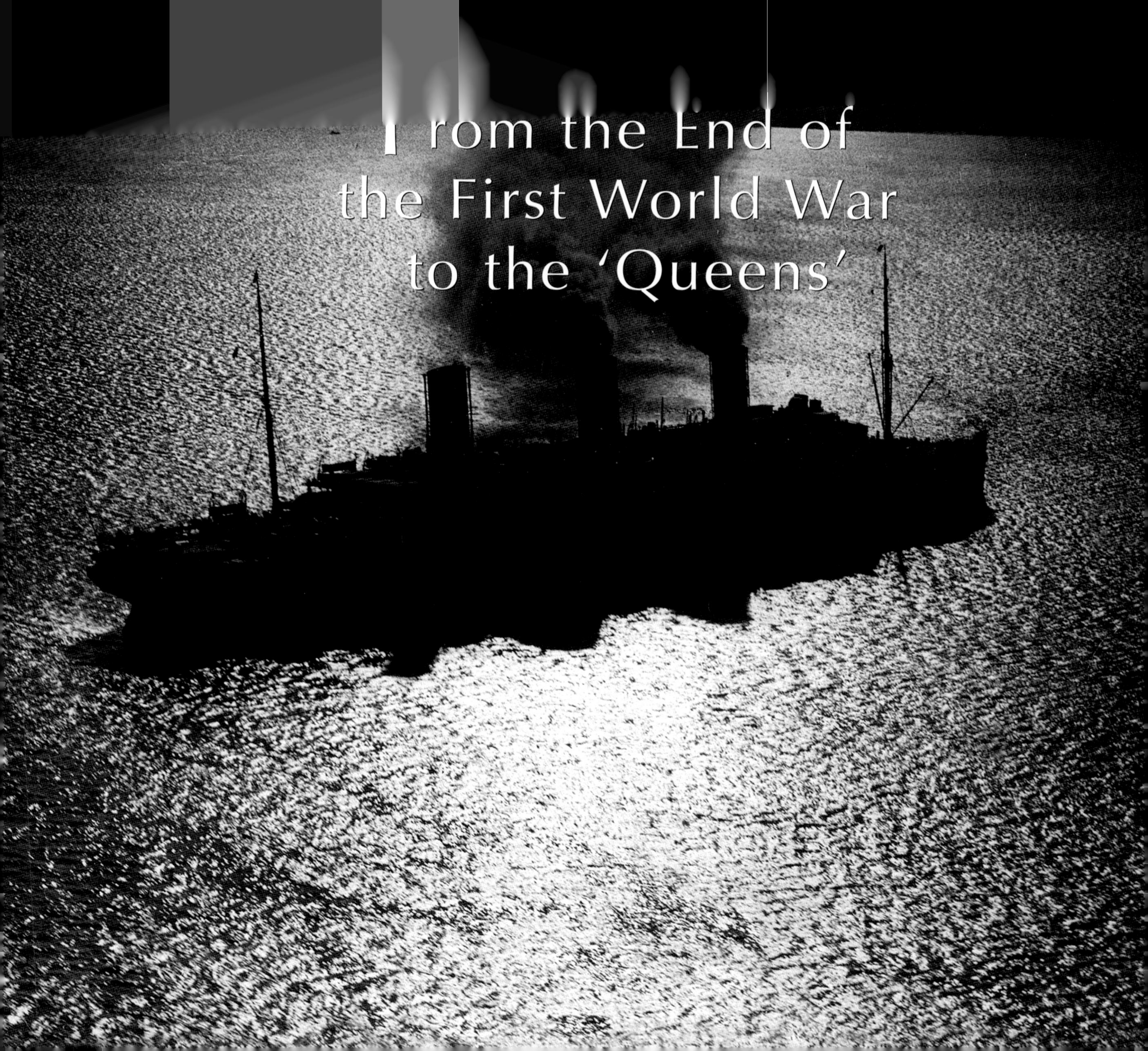

Previous page: In happier times, *Berengaria* from the air, as she approaches Cherbourg en route to New York.

Above: Twenty-two ships were lost in the First World War and Cunard had lost *Lusitania*, one of their 'Big Three' liners. German war reparations meant that they acquired *Imperator*, the Hamburg Amerika liner. Renamed *Berengaria*, she became the ideal running mate for *Aquitania* and the old *Mauretania*.

Left: Photographed at Southampton, *c.*1930. *Berengaria* was sold for scrapping in 1939 after being condemned due to the hazardous state of her electrical wiring, which had caught fire one time too many.

As the First World War drew to a close, trade on the North Atlantic returned to normal. By 1922, *Mauretania*, *Aquitania* and *Berengaria* became the most popular ships on the Atlantic, and all classes of passengers flocked to them. Their elegant, country house style interiors were extremely popular.

Emigration had played a huge part in the growth of the company but all this had changed by the mid-1920s. The huge reduction in numbers of immigrants to the USA meant that companies like Cunard had to find new passengers. Tourism was beginning to become more affordable and Cunard built some ships and converted others specifically to cater for this market. Tourist third-class was designed for the person who wanted to travel cheaply and in pleasant surroundings.

In 1923, the *Franconia* (II) entered service. She left on her maiden voyage from Liverpool on 23 June of that year, and she headed for New York. During her lifetime, she was chartered by the Furness-Bermuda line for cruising and also undertook one of Cunard's first world cruises – taking in a total of thirty-seven ports and 41,727 miles. She survived the Second World War and was the HQ ship for the Yalta, Crimea, conference between President Roosevelt of the United States, Russia's leader, Stalin, and Britain's Prime Minister, Churchill.

Until 1925, Cunard was rebuilding its fleet, which had been decimated during the First World War. Just prior to *Franconia*'s introduction the 'A' class ships were added: *Andania* (II), *Antonia*, *Ausonia* (II) and *Aurania* (III). Just after this *Ascania* (II), *Alaunia* (II) and *Carinthia* (II) completed the post-war building.

In 1926 Cunard started making plans for their newest 'monster ships'. Their three grand old ladies, *Berengaria*, *Mauretania* and *Aquitania*, were starting to show their age, and thoughts turned to new ships to replace them. Rumours were circulating that the French Line was planning a new superliner whose 'beauty and speed would surpass all ships currently sailing on the Atlantic'. The German Norddeutscher Lloyd line was also planning to build two superliners called *Bremen* and *Europa*. Upon entering service, the German ships took the Blue Riband from *Mauretania*, a record she had held since 1908.

On 28 May 1930 John Brown's in Clydebank was informed that they had been awarded the contract for the first of Cunard's two new superliners. They gave her the build number 534. After initial problems with insurance and dry-docking arrangements, the work on hull 534 continued without a hitch until the end of 1931. The American stock market crash in 1929 caused most of the economies of the developed world to go into decline and so began the Great Depression. Cunard's *Berengaria* had had the first

Above: In 1924, Southampton docks acquired a floating dock capable of lifting 60,000 tons. Here, *Aquitania* has been lifted clear of the water for a refit.

Below: An aerial view of *Aquitania* in the Ocean Dock, Southampton. Originally called the White Star Dock, the name was changed in the 1920s as ships of other lines were using it regularly. Next to *Aquitania* can be seen the Trafalgar Graving Dock and the floating dry dock.

Above: Vellavia, one of the 1918 cargo ships, at Liverpool. She was in Cunard service until 1931 but was scrapped in Tokyo in 1959 after an eventful career which involved being seized by Argentina during the Second World War and being scuttled in Porto Vecchio Bay in 1951.

Below: Albania was the first new ship built after the war for Cunard. Intended for the Canadian service, she was never hugely successful and was sold in 1930 after five years lay-up. She became the *California* for Liberia Triestina.

Above: The sisters *Scythia* and *Samaria* were the first passenger liners built for the company after the war. *Scythia*, shown here on the right, was built at Glasgow but fitted out at Barrow-in-Furness. She was used as a troopship during the Second World War and scrapped at Inverkeithing in 1958.

Below: Liverpool Landing Stage, *c.*1925 with RMS *Samaria*.

ever floating stock market installed a short while before the 'crash' and wealthy clients on board had watched some of their fortunes slip away. By 1931, businesses were failing, huge numbers of people were unemployed and others just did not have the money for luxuries like travel. The United States also closed its ports to most emigrants – the shipping companies' biggest revenue. The shipping companies were really feeling the pinch.

Cunard was in a perilous situation and found itself unable to afford to continue construction of their 80,000-ton liner. By Christmas 1931, work had stopped on hull 534. Cunard could not afford to run their services and build such a luxurious liner in the midst of a recession. The workers at John Brown's were laid off and it was a very bleak Christmas indeed.

For the next two years, hull 534 stood like a massive monument to the Depression. David Kirkwood, MP for Clydebank, became convinced that if work on the ship was restarted, then it would provide a kick-start for the economy, and get thousands of people – not just in Clydebank – back to work. After consultation with various bodies, including the Prince of Wales, the Government produced the Weir Report. The report concluded that it would be in the country's interests to restart work on hull 534, and also that the Cunard Line should merge with the ailing White Star Line to create the Cunard White Star Line Ltd. The Government planned to provide Cunard White Star with subsidies and a working loan.

Right, above and below: Laconia was built at Swan Hunter's to the same design as *Scythia*. Used for cruising in the 1930s, she was sunk in 1942 by torpedo while carrying 1,800 Italian prisoners of war. Rescued by German U-boats, these were subsequently attacked and the survivors left to their fates. She is shown here at Manilla (above) and Cristobal (below).

Above: Four new sisters, the 'A' liners, were built for the Canadian route. *Andania, Antonia, Ausonia* and *Aurania* became popular cabin-class ships, both luxurious and relatively cheap to travel on.

Far left: The message on the back of this photograph states that Budne was a passenger on board *Ausonia* en route from Liverpool to Montreal and going on to British Columbia.

Left: Lancastria entered service as *Tyrrhenia* in 1922. Originally nicknamed the 'soup tureen', her name was changed to *Lancastria* in 1924. In 1940, *Lancastria* was evacuating troops and civilians from St Nazaire when she was bombed and sunk. It was unknown how many people were on board but the number was over 5,000. Of those, *Lancastria* became a coffin for upwards of 3,000 souls. Shown here when cruising, she is leaving Lerwick in the Shetland Islands.

Above and above right:
The tender at Liverpool was *Skirmisher* (above left), while at Cherbourg the tenders were specially built in 1924. Shown here (above right) is *Lotharingia,* while the other tender was called *Alsatia.*

Right: Lifeboat drill on *Lancastria, c.*1930.

Top left: Franconia and *Carinthia* spent much time cruising. *Carinthia* is shown here at the newly completed Sydney Harbour Bridge.

Top right: While *Franconia* is dressed overall on a visit to Madras, India.

Bottom left: Some of the cargo vessels were also being made redundant. *Brescia* was sold off for scrapping and is here at Preston for breaking up.

Bottom right: Replacements for the older cargo vessels included *Bothnia*, built at Sunderland by J.L. Thompson. She was used on the Mediterranean cargo run. Here she is in Liverpool's dock system.

The workers triumphantly marched through the gates of John Brown's on 3 April 1934 to resume work. Hull 534 had been kept in such good condition that it passed a Lloyds inspection with flying colours. Work continued uneventfully until the launch of the liner in September of that year.

On a cold, rainy day on 26 September 1934, King George V and Queen Mary arrived to perform the launch ceremony. The Queen cut the ribbon and the new British superliner RMS *Queen Mary* slid into the water for the first time.

CUNARD WHITE STAR LIMITED AND
JOHN BROWN & COMPANY, LIMITED

LAUNCH OF S.S. No. 534

from Clydebank Shipyard
on Wednesday, 26th September, 1934,
at 3 p.m.

This Card admits ONE PERSON.
It is to be shewn at Entrance Gate, also on entering the
Launching Platform, and given up later on entering Mould
Loft, where Tea will be served.

Table M1   Seat No. 3

NOT TRANSFERABLE

Top and above: In the late 1920s, plans were under way to replace the Edwardian trio on the express route.

Above right: Once the decision to retire the express trio was made, the design work of what would become *Queen Mary* started. She, and a sister, would take over the express run to New York from Southampton. Here is a ticket for the Royal Box for the launch of 534, as *Queen Mary's* hull was known.

Normandie, the 80,000grt French superliner, took to the North Atlantic a few months later. She was the most beautiful and fastest liner built to that date. On Queen Mary's birthday, 27 May 1936, RMS *Queen Mary* left Southampton on her maiden voyage. She was a party-ship all the way to New York, all one class for this voyage. Although not as stunning as *Normandie*, she had extremely beautiful interiors. Gone were the days of the country house interior. Even the third-class section of the *Queen Mary* was better than many second-class areas in most ships. The emigrant days were gone and Cunard had to attract tourists and business people into third-class.

After *Queen Mary's* maiden voyage, thoughts then turned to her sister ship and John Brown's was awarded the contract for this too. Hull 552's keel was laid in December 1936 on the same slipway that had held her sister for so long.

The new breed of ocean liners began to influence art and architecture on both sides of the Atlantic. Many Art Deco buildings were based on the long, fluid lines of the ocean liner. The interiors of these buildings reflected the interiors of the ocean liners too, with beautiful artwork, imaginative use of wood and lighting; and soon other ideas generated by the ocean liner arrived on dry land, and were developed into the must-have interiors of the smart set.

As work progressed on the newest Cunarder, the dark clouds of war hung over the horizon. Launched in September 1938, just after the *Mauretania* (II) the new liner was given the name *Queen Elizabeth*. It was announced by the Prime Minster, Neville Chamberlain, that Britain was now at war with Germany on 3 September 1939. The *Queen Mary* was already at sea and Cunard decided that she should

Above: Construction was halted on *Queen Mary* in the midst of the Depression and it was only the merger of Cunard and White Star that saw it started again. Photographed by RAF reconnaissance plane, *Queen Mary* is being fitted out soon after her launch at Clydebank.

Above left: RMS *Mauretania*, resplendent in white at Southampton in June 1933.

Left: RMS *Aquitania*, at Calshot, Southampton.

head for a safe and neutral port – New York. She joined the French liner *Normandie*, already safely berthed on the Hudson. After much debate, it was decided to prepare the *Queen Elizabeth* to a minimum standard and send her across to join her sister *Queen Mary* in New York. The *Queen Elizabeth* made her maiden voyage under total secrecy in March 1940. In fact, it was so secret that when she appeared in New York, no one but a few Cunard staff knew what this massive liner was. She was soon to be New York's biggest tourist attraction!

Later in March 1940, the *Queen Mary* was called up for war service, followed by the *Queen Elizabeth* soon after. Both were converted into troopships and sailed around the world, moving troops to where they were needed most.

During the Second World War, a total of seventeen Cunard vessels served as troopships or Armed Merchant Cruisers. This included the two Queens, the *Laurentic* (II), *Franconia* (II) and *Britannic* (III). The Queens started ferrying troops between Australia and Egypt, then switched to the North Atlantic run after America entered the war. One

of the company's first war losses was the *Lancastria*, sunk at St Nazaire in 1940 with the loss of over 3,000 crew, soldiers and evacuated civilians.

In 1942, one of the most tragic events in the *Queen Mary*'s history happened when she rammed HMS *Curacoa*, a cruiser which regularly escorted ships from the Irish coast to the safety of the Clyde. On 2 October 1942, she was escorting the *Queen Mary* into port when a navigation error occurred and she ran into the path of the massive liner. The *Queen Mary* sliced a large chunk off the *Curacoa*'s stern and the cruiser sank, killing 338 crew. The survivors were picked up by the other ships in the escort group as the *Queen Mary* was under strict instructions not to stop for anything.

Both the *Queen Mary* and *Queen Elizabeth* kept having their troop-carrying capacity increased. Initially they carried 2,500 troops, but after America entered the war, they were converted to carry as many as 16,000. *Queen Mary* still holds the world record for the largest number of people moved at one time with over 16,000 passengers and crew on one wartime voyage.

Posters advertising the Canadian service, both showing *Ascania*.

Aquitania at New York.

RMS *Samaria* leaving Liverpool at night.

Until *Queen Mary*, *Berengaria* was the largest Cunarder.

RMS *Laconia*, the first liner of her size to pass through the Panama Canal.

Equipped especially for cruising, *Franconia* was a 'palace of rest and recreation'.

RMS *Mauretania*, the world's fastest liner for over twenty years.

At Calshot, Southampton, RMS *Aquitania*, the 'World's Wonder Ship'.

Above: Leaving John Brown's, 26 March 1936. On her way down the Clyde, *Queen Mary* was spun by a gust of wind and jammed across the river. A few hours later she was pulled off the mudbank and continued her first ever trip.

Opposite page
Top left: RMS *Queen Mary* sailing down the Clyde past RMS *Davaar*, PS *Talisman*, the Southampton tug *Romsey* and the Caledonian Steam Packet steamer TS *Atalanta* immediately before her sea trials in March 1936.

Middle left: With the merger of Cunard and White Star, a rationalisation of the fleet was undertaken and many ships went to the breakers, including *Mauretania*, shown here docked in Rosyth for final breaking up.

Bottom left: The combined fleet had three of the four largest ships in the world and *Majestic*, acquired from White Star, was sent to the breakers in 1936, soon after the *Titanic*'s sister, RMS *Olympic*, had been broken up. Here, *Majestic*, once the largest steamer in the world, awaits her fate at Thorneycroft's in Southampton.

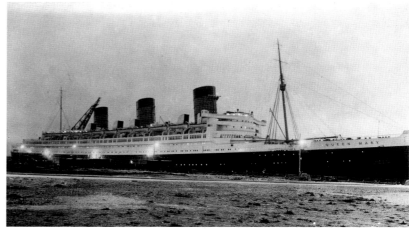

Top: RMS *Queen Mary* in dry dock at Southampton, April 1936.

Above: Painted by Charles Pears, and hung on board *Queen Mary*, this is *Mauretania* passing under the Forth Rail Bridge on the way to Ward's at Rosyth.

THE OCEAN DOCK, SOUTHAMPTON.

CUNARD WHITE STAR LINE *Cruises*

Above: Majestic had a short reprieve, becoming a training ship for the Navy but was destroyed by fire in 1940. Here she is seen in better times with her sister *Berengaria* in Southampton's Ocean Dock.

Below: In an effort to make them pay through the Depression, other ships, like *Britannic* and *Franconia*, were sent cruising.

Above: Doric, shown here, lasted in joint ownership for two years before she was rammed by a French cargo ship called *Formigny* and sent to the breakers as uneconomical to repair. Her lifeboats are beginning to be launched in this view from the Orient liner *Orion* almost immediately after the collision.

Below: A Cunarder unloading cargo in London Docks.

Cunard Cruising

Reproduced by courtesy of "The Ill

PLEASURE-CRUISE LIFE IN A LUXURY LINER: THE DELIGHTFUL NEW FORM OF HOLIDAY-MAKING BY OCEAN TOURS AT ALL SEASONS OF THE Y

The vogue of ocean touring has increased enormously, and during the coming season this new type of holiday will doubtless prove even more popular. Though the great shipping concerns which run fortnightly trips to the Mediterranean, Atlantic Isles, and Norwegian Fiords do not make a large profit from them, nevertheless they are keeping ships and crews employed and ducating thousands of people to realise what a wonderful life can be enjoyed in a well-appointed British liner; moreover, the money spent goes largely into British pockets. Our illustration shows the Cunard cruising liner "Lancastria" (17,000 tons) gently steaming

in the Straits of Gibraltar and affording passengers their first glimpse of the Rock. To give some idea of the amenities in magnificent floating hotel, we illustrate the upper deck busy with sports and pastimes, organised by the expert sports staff board known as Cruise Directors. Naturally, all these pastimes would not always be proceeding simultaneously. Besides the items show there are regular fancy-dress dances on the sports deck when cruising in warm climes; bridge and whist drives, and athletic aquatic sports. For the studious there is the free library, stocked with 2000 books. Lower down in the ship are two or more beautiful

The inside of a Cunard cruising liner: a cutaway drawing of *Lancastria*.

KITCHENS OF A CRUISING LINER

THE CREW OF A 17,000-TON CRUISING LINER

LING PASSENGERS TO SEE THE SIGHTS OF FOREIGN LANDS, WHILE ENJOYING ALL THE AMENITIES ABOARD THEIR OWN "FLOATING HOTEL."

ed dining-saloons providing good and wholesome food to suit every taste. Unseen by most of the tourists there is another side picture—the great kitchens, the cooled store-rooms containing vast quantities of food-stuffs, the linen store, and the bakery. The shop publishes a free newspaper of world news received by wireless, and also the ship's newspaper with all the latest happenings floating town. Experts arrange excursions to view the sights ashore. In this way you see the world without having to sleep in ashore, or eat food that perhaps may not suit your English digestion, and you have not to be continually packing and unpacking

your baggage. In the numerous luxurious public rooms you can have a drink, a game of cards, a laze or a read, and write letters. In the gymnasium you can do your "daily dozen." The ship is large and there is plenty of room for all. It is well found and a good sea-boat. Though the cost of oil-fuel, port dues, and tender charges have to be taken into consideration by the owners, nevertheless the ocean tourist can enjoy all the aforesaid amenities, and see wonderful new sights in foreign lands for little more than one pound per day.—[Drawn Specially for "The Illustrated London News" by G. H. Davis.]

CUNARD WHITE STAR LIMITED AND
JOHN BROWN & COMPANY, LIMITED

STEAMER &
LAUNCHING
PLATFORM

LAUNCH OF S.S. No. 552

from Clydebank Shipyard
on Tuesday, 27th September, 1938,
at 3.15 p.m.

This Card entitles ONE PERSON to go on board the Turbine Steamer "DUCHESS OF HAMILTON," at Bridge Wharf (South Side), Glasgow. The Steamer will leave for Clydebank Shipyard at 1.30 p.m.

The Card should be shewn on entering Launching Platform and at the gangway on returning to Steamer after the Launch.

The Turbine Steamer "DUCHESS OF HAMILTON" will leave Shipyard, West Side of Dock at 4.15 p.m., and Tea will be served on the return journey.

DRESS: MORNING DRESS   NOT TRANSFERABLE

CAMMELL LAIRD & COMPANY LIMITED.

LAUNCH OF T.S.S. "MAURETANIA"

By LADY BATES

On THURSDAY 28th July, 1938

ENTRANCE TO YARD GREEN LANE GATE

ADMIT ONE
TO
PLATFORM only

VISITORS SHOULD BE IN THEIR PLACES NOT LATER THAN 11-45 A.M.

This card to be shown at the entrance to the Works and at the entrance to the Platform.

Cameras must not be brought into the Shipyard.

NO SPACE FOR PARKING CARS AVAILABLE.

Dinner
May 12th 1939

To commemorate the Atlantic voyage
of Their Majesties
King George and Queen Elizabeth
to visit Canada & the United States
and the
Second Anniversary of Their Coronation

Far left: Mauretania entered service just a month before war started. Dressed overall, she is berthed here before her maiden voyage with the Isle of Man Steam Packet Co.'s *Lady of Mann* in the background.

Top left: By 1938, a new sister for *Queen Mary* had been launched. The *Queen Elizabeth* was to enter service in May 1940 and would inaugurate the two-ship weekly service, but war intervened.

Middle and bottom: In 1938, another famous Cunarder was launched too. Built on the Mersey, the second ship to carry the name *Mauretania* was destined to become almost as famous as the first.

Right: Immediately before the war in May 1939, King George V and Queen Elizabeth travelled in the *Queen Mary* on their tour of Canada and the United States

Opposite page

Top left: At the outbreak of war, the *Queen Mary* was en route to New York with her biggest ever peacetime passenger complement. In wartime she was to carry many, many more than her designed capacity, eventually holding the record for carrying the largest number of people at one go, over 16,000 passengers and crew. Very soon she was painted grey and sporting a gun at her stern.

Top right: Leaving the fitting-out basin at Clydebank in March 1940 is the *Queen Elizabeth*, at the time the world's largest moving object. Under threat of bombing by the Germans, she sailed into the Firth of Clyde to perform basic sea trials and then set off for the USA, away from the Nazi threat.

Bottom left: For a matter of weeks the three largest ships in the world were berthed next to each other in New York. Soon the *Queen Mary* left the French Line's *Normandie* and the *Queen Elizabeth* behind and travelled to Australia to begin the conversion to a troopship.

Middle right: All of the Cunard ships were called up for military service, and converted to troopships or Armed Merchant Cruisers. *Mauretania* is shown here in Sydney, Australia, the crowd of white-jacketed stewards at her bow clashing terribly with her dull grey paintwork.

Bottom right: Soldiers wait to board *Franconia*.

This page: By the end of the war, *Queen Mary* and *Queen Elizabeth* had carried over a million troops to battle. But their war was not over. For months afterwards both ships carried GI brides and servicemen back to their home countries. *Queen Mary* is shown entering Southampton for the first time since August 1939 on 11 August 1945.

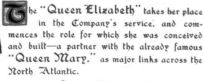

Top left: Aquitania was the only four stacker to survive two world wars. She shouldn't have lasted so long, being destined to go to the breakers in 1940 when the *Queen Elizabeth* came into service. Instead, she survived until 1949 and is shown here at New York in mid-1945.

Left: The first Cunarder to return from war service was the *Queen Elizabeth*, making her post-war maiden voyage in October 1946. Shown here is a certificate given to a maiden-voyage passenger.

Top right: During the war *Queen Elizabeth* carried over 800,000 soldiers and travelled almost half-a-million miles.

Above: Built during the war, *Valacia* is shown here at Cape Town. She was sold out of Cunard service in 1950, being purchased by Charles Hill of Bristol and renamed *New York City*.

Chapter Four

The Post-War Years

LAUNCH OF THE

T.S.S. "PARTHIA"

FOR

Cunard White Star, Limited

NAMED BY

Lady Brooke

TUESDAY, 25th, FEBRUARY, 1947

Previous page: Cunard's first cargo/passenger liners designed to carry first-class passengers only were *Media* and *Parthia*. *Media* was built at John Brown's and *Parthia* at Harland & Wolff, Belfast.

Above left: Cunard's first post-war new build was *Asia* in 1947. Destined for the US cargo service, she could carry twelve first-class passengers. Her sister ship was *Arabia*.

Above: Perhaps the most famous of the new Cunarders was the *Caronia*. At a time of extreme austerity and rationing, she was built to be a luxury cruising liner. Her funnel was the largest of any ship and is shown here being fitted on 27 August 1948.

Left: The menu given to guests for the launch of the *Parthia* at Belfast.

When the Second World War ended with the Japanese capitulation, Cunard had lost six ships, and had had three sold to the Government for use as Navy depot and stores ships. The war did not end immediately for the shipping lines as the millions of Commonwealth and American troops had to be repatriated. The big ships, including the Queens, *Mauretania* (II) and *Aquitania,* were kept in military service with the *Queen Elizabeth* being released first from returning troops home and taking GI Brides across to their new homelands. *Aquitania,* destined to be scrapped in 1940 when the *Queen Elizabeth* was introduced, was the only four-funnelled ship to be involved in both the First and Second World Wars. She soldiered on until her last voyage in December 1949, and was then scrapped at Faslane, Scotland in 1950. She had sailed 3 million miles and carried more than 1.2 million passengers.

Queen Elizabeth's first fare-paying maiden voyage was six years late and began in October 1946 as she sailed triumphantly from war-ravaged Britain for the United States on her first commercial voyage. The *Queen Mary* returned to the Atlantic within the year, making her maiden post-war voyage in July 1947. *Ascania* (II) was also refurbished. *Asia* (II) and *Arabia* (III) were the first cargo ships built post war with the cargo/passenger liners *Media* and *Parthia* (II) providing first-class accommodation only, being built in 1948.

For dollar-earning potential *Caronia* (II) was built in 1949. Designed as a dual-role cruise/passenger ship, she was painted in a fetching green livery. In winter she sailed out of New York on extended cruises and in summer was used as a passenger ship on the Atlantic Ferry.

For a few years life returned to its pre-war normality on the Atlantic. The Queens were proving a great success, providing the weekly express service they were designed for. They were now the biggest, fastest ships on the Atlantic by default, as their competitors, like the *Normandie, Rex* and *Bremen,* had been destroyed during the Second World War.

Even in dry dock, she was an impressive ship. Painted in four shades of green, she was stunning to look at as well as sail in. *Caronia* made her last Cunard voyage in 1969 and was sold to Universal Lines Inc., who sold her on to the Star Shipping Co., who intended using her for cruising again. The company went into liquidation and she was laid up in New York then sold for scrapping at Taiwan, but she never reached there, being wrecked at Guam in a tropical storm.

Cunard Freight Services

Top left: Cunard were building up the freight services again and new builds included *Assyria, Alsatia* and *Andria,* with the latter two shown here. Other new cargo ships included *Pavia, Lycia* and *Phrygia,* one a year from 1953.

Top right: Cunard's 174th ship was the first of four sisters, *Saxonia,* and she joined an expanding fleet of new vessels.

Bottom left: The Cunard fleet, c.1955.

Bottom right: Saxonia was renamed *Carmania* in 1963 and was used for Mediterranean fly-cruise holidays.

After the war though, America was worried about its troop-carrying capacity in the event of another major conflict. They had had to borrow the Queens and other tonnage from Britain in order to move troops and cargo quickly during the war and this was not an arrangement America wanted. They decided to build their own superliner, and by 1952, the SS *United States* had made her maiden voyage. Her speed eclipsed the Queens, and she spectacularly took the Blue Riband from the *Queen Mary*. Integral to the *United States*' design was the ability to be converted into a troopship when needed within forty-eight hours. Her interiors were very up-to-date, and she started taking some of the North Atlantic passenger trade away from the Queens.

In December 1949, in a corporate reshuffle and simplification, Cunard Line took over the assets of Cunard White Star Ltd and White Star as an organisation ceased to exist. Its last two ships, *Georgic* and *Britannic*, still flew the company livery of buff funnel until their scrapping.

During 1953, the Cunard board decided that it was time to replace some of their ageing Canadian liners. These older ships, the youngest of which was over twenty years old, included *Franconia* (II) and *Scythia* (II). Four new 'sisters' were built at John Brown's shipyard on the Clyde. The new ships were *Sylvania* (II), *Ivernia* (II), *Saxonia* (II) and *Carinthia* (II).

By 1960, Cunard had a fleet of ten passenger ships on the North Atlantic, as well as a fleet of cargo ships and life still looked relatively rosy. The passenger ships were still generating large profits. The *United States* was a threat, but there was enough trade on the Atlantic to keep everyone in business. Only one problem clouded a good future for the liners, and that was the jet…

Above: The second of the quartet was *Ivernia*, here making her first call at Le Havre, westbound on 8 December 1956.

Below: Carinthia, the third sister, was introduced in June 1956, making her maiden voyage to Montreal on the 27th of that month.

Top left: At the same time as the new quartet were introduced, *Scythia*, one of the pre-war ships, was heading for the breakers yard, being scrapped in 1958.

Top right: Carinthia was sold in 1968 to the Sitmar Line, becoming *Fairsea*, only recently being scrapped after a long career, including a time with Princess Cruises as *Fair Princess.*

Bottom left: The last two survivors of the White Star fleet were *Georgic* and *Britannic. Georgic* had been sold to the Ministry of War Transport after she was bombed in Egypt in 1943. Used as a troopship she was hired back to Cunard for a period in the early 1950s and was scrapped in 1956.

Bottom right: Britannic was the last ship to sail in White Star livery and she was a successful cruise ship and liner all through the 1950s. Engine problems saw her end her career in 1960 and she headed for Scotland to be scrapped in December of that year.

Chapter Five

The Company's Fortunes Change

Top right: … and on the principal of 'if you can't beat them, join them', Cunard got into the airline business in conjunction with BOAC and in their own right as Cunard Eagle Airways. This is a BOAC Cunard Vickers VC-10.

Bottom left: In winter, ships like *Queen Mary* and *Queen Elizabeth* were travelling with fewer than 200 passengers on occasion.

Bottom right: In 1965 another famous name left Southampton for the last time and went to the breakers yard at Inverkeithing. Painted in green in 1962 and sent cruising, *Mauretania* became increasingly unprofitable. It was only a matter of time and it is surprising she lasted so long. She is shown here passing under the Verrazano Narrows Bridge in the twilight of her career.

Previous Page: Strikes were also having a huge impact on profits and helped generate huge losses for Cunard. The 1966 seamen's strike probably cost the British merchant marine more than it achieved for the strikers. Cunard shore staff watch as *Caronia*, the first ship to sail after the end of the strike, passes in tow of the tug/tender *Calshot*, which still survives (just) in Southampton. *Queen Elizabeth*, in the distance, sailed later in the day on 2 July 1966.

Top left: Air travel was beginning to have a huge impact on passenger numbers by the late 1950s…

The jet was proving more of a success than had been initially thought. During the Second World War, technology and flight endurance had improved to such an extent that an aircraft was able to cross the Atlantic in eleven hours. By 1953, the de Havilland Comet, the world's first jet airliner, was in service. Until the introduction of the Boeing 707, Atlantic air travel was mainly by flying boat or by piston-engined aircraft. The 707 revolutionised air travel. It was possible to fly the Atlantic in under eight hours. For those who could afford it, eight hours above the weather in relative luxury, compared with four days in a rolling ship, was now the way to travel. The rich and famous began deserting the liners for the jet.

During the early 1960s strikes became a major problem for the shipping companies. They delayed sailings and timetables had to be changed. Passengers were not pleased by this, and it contributed to the popularity of the jet. Why travel by the unreliable strike-prone liner when one could travel by air? On the principle of, 'if you can't beat them, join them', Cunard acquired a 60 per cent stake in Eagle Airways.

Cunard started to send their ships cruising in order to try to make up for lost revenue. *Saxonia* (II) and *Ivernia* (II) were altered for cruising and renamed *Carmania* (II) and *Franconia* (III), respectively. The Queens were sent cruising to the Mediterranean, Canary Islands and Bermuda, but this was not a success. They were too big, weren't air conditioned and used too much fuel. With winter sailings carrying less than 200 passengers, the Queens were operating at a huge loss. In the end, it was decided to sell them off to the highest bidder. The *Queen Mary* was first to go in October 1967, when she sailed to Long Beach, California, to become a floating hotel, museum and conference centre. To this day, she remains there. The *Queen Elizabeth*

Above left: At the breakers yard at Inverkeithing, *Mauretania*, still in green, is not a pretty sight as she is dismantled.

Above: One always prefers to remember ships in happier times. *Mauretania* at New York, 1960.

was not quite so fortunate. She was sold to a Philadelphia business consortium in 1968, which planned to turn her into the star attraction in their Seven Wonders of the World theme park, near Delaware (with the *Queen Elizabeth* being the eighth!). This fell through after it was found her draught was too deep for her to sail upriver. Then she went to Port Everglades, but after a change in control of the Port Authority, she was then sold back to Cunard, who again tried to find a new buyer. Shipping magnate C.Y. Tung, of Hong Kong, bought her with plans to turn her into a floating university. Just as the conversion was nearing completion in 1972, fires broke out at various points on board. After futile attempts to dowse the flames, she was left to burn out. She rolled over and capsized. Her wreckage was left rusting and half submerged until 1974 when it was salvaged down to the keel.

Cunard started selling off the rest of its fleet, to reduce the heavy losses which it was incurring. *Caronia* (II), *Sylvania* (II) and *Carinthia* (III) were all sold. *Carinthia* (III) and *Sylvania* (II) were sold to the Sitmar Line, which was later to become part of Princess Cruises.

1962 saw the French build a new liner called *France*. *France* was the most sophisticated and modern liner at sea – even eclipsing t he *United States*. The *France* was taking nearly all the first-class passengers away from the Queens, and also a large slice of the business too. It was with competition in mind that Cunard took the brave step to sell the Queens and consider building a new liner more in tune with the demands of the day. In the days when the jet was so obviously the way to travel, some considered this to be rather foolhardy. Cunard thought that a ship the size of the Queens, which could be converted into a cruise ship in winter, but take to the North Atlantic in summer, would be the answer.

A design was formulated for a new liner code-named Q3, but as time went on, it was realised that such a large ship would be uneconomical. The estimated building costs were escalating, and with the financial situation Cunard was in, it was realised that Q3 was financially unviable.

With the Q3 project scuppered, Cunard turned their attention to a new, smaller design – Q4. Q4 was much smaller than Q3 and was truly designed for both North Atlantic service and for cruising. She was also a lot lighter – a consideration for a ship that was designed to traverse the Panama Canal. Her superstructure was built of aluminium. The contract for her construction was again given to

The company's fortunes were in decline and in 1966 it was announced that the *Queen Mary* was to retire the following year. Looking out from a derelict warehouse in Southampton at the *Queen Mary*.

Left top: Queen Elizabeth, despite a huge refit in 1966, was destined to go the following year.

Left middle and bottom: Sailing from New York, *Queen Elizabeth* made her final Cunard voyage in November 1968. She made a farewell cruise to the Canary Islands and was then sold to interests in Florida. Unable to pay their bills, the ship was sold again to C.Y. Tung and disastrously burned out in Hong Kong Harbour in 1972.

Above: Looking down from the crow's nest on *Queen Mary.*

Top left: The crew of HMS *Wakeful* salute the *Queen Mary* as she sails for a new life as a museum and hotel in Long Beach, California.

Top right: As passenger services declined rapidly, Cunard was still operating many cargo ships, including the third *Alaunia*, shown here on her maiden arrival in New York in October 1960.

Bottom left: While traditional passenger services were in terminal decline, Cunard were building a new cruise/passenger ship called Q4. Launched by Her Majesty the Queen, she was the last John Brown-built Cunard ocean liner. Built with a mainly aluminium superstructure, she was also pre-fabricated in sections and welded together.

Bottom right: Queen Elizabeth 2 in the fitting out basin at John Brown's in early September 1968.

Left: QE2's interiors were indeed state-of-the-art and perfectly in tune with the times.

Below: In 1967 Cunard tried a novel experiment in conjunction with British European Airways. They hired a hovercraft and used it on fly-drive cruises out of Gibraltar. Loading of the SRN.6 hovercraft (built at Cowes on the Isle of Wight) at Gibraltar.

John Brown's in Clydebank, and on 30 December 1964, the contract was signed for the new liner. She was given the build number 736. Her keel was laid on 5 July 1965 (4 July – the traditional keel-laying day of Cunard vessels – was a Sunday).

In May 1969, after many problems, the *Queen Elizabeth 2*, as the new liner was named by Her Majesty the Queen, sailed on her maiden voyage. She formed part of the fleet with *Franconia* (III) and *Carmania* (II). *Carmania* (II) and *Franconia* (III) were to make occasional transatlantic voyages, but were used mainly for cruising.

The *QE2's* interior design was futuristic and ultra-modern. She had 'space-age' seating in the Queen's Room and the most up-to-date wall coverings. Again, Cunard used the finest designers and materials to create a stunning, modern vessel.

QE2's exterior caused a stir in the late 1960s. Her profile, and futuristic-style funnel were revolutionary at the time, and came in for a lot of criticism. A popular view was that such a revolutionary design would not be accepted by the public. Her funnel wasn't even painted in the traditional orange-red of Cunard. Since that time, however, *QE2's* profile and funnel have become her trademark – instantly recognisable – and loved by many.

With the jet liner becoming more popular, the rich and famous were looking for more enjoyable and comfortable alternatives to aeroplane travel. *QE2* filled a niche market. She could provide rest and relaxation in the most luxurious surroundings. She could also provide anonymity from the stresses and strains of fame. In the fast pace of life in the early 1970s, stars and royalty flocked to her because she provided a comfortable alternative on the North Atlantic route.

Cunard and the French Line negotiated a deal whereby *QE2* and *France* would cross the Atlantic during alternate weeks in the summer. This reduced competition for both lines and made both ships more economically viable (it also gave passengers a chance to do a return journey on two very different, but equally glamorous liners!).

In 1970 Cunard stopped its North Atlantic cargo service when it terminated its contract with United Dominions Leasing Ltd, and returned their leased ship *Scotia* (II). This ship was the first Cunarder with an engine room controlled from the Bridge. The *Media* (II) and *Parthia* (III) were then transferred to Brocklebank Line. They were renamed *Mahronda* and *Manipur* for the company's eastern service.

Owing to continuing financial difficulties and the almost total demise of passenger trade on the North Atlantic, the entire share capital of the Cunard Steamship Co. was purchased by Trafalgar House Investments Ltd for £26 million on 24 August 1971. Trafalgar House owned 260 companies world wide, including hotels, civil engineering firms and property. A clause in Cunard's Articles of Association did not allow the company to be sold to foreign

Above: The hovercraft being taken aboard *Sylvania* at Southampton in early 1967. The experiment wasn't a success and the hovercraft was returned in April 1967.

Above right: The 1970s saw a new series of smaller cruise ships intended for Caribbean service. *Cunard Ambassador*, built in Rotterdam in 1971 was burned out in 1974. The ship was sold off and converted to a cattle carrier. Her sister *Cunard Adventurer* is shown here at Southampton in 1971.

investors, and as Trafalgar House was a British company, this was favourable for both sides.

In a declining passenger market, Cunard decided to direct its attentions to its cargo trade. Eight new container ships were ordered under the new management company of Cunard-Brocklebank Ltd. This company integrated the management of the Moss and Brocklebank fleets and Cunard's Atlantic cargo fleet. The new Cunard ships were completed between 1972 and 1973. Added to this were seven deadweight oil product carriers – *Luminiere, Luminetta, Lumen, Luminous, Lustrous, Lucigen,* and *Luxor.*

Cunard sold *Franconia* and *Carmania* in 1971, but already had two new ships under construction. The *Cunard Adventurer* and *Cunard Ambassador* were acquired from the Overseas National Airways in the early stages of building. Overseas National Airways had intended to enter the cruise market in the United States and use their planes to take passengers to these ships; but unfortunately, their ambitions were hampered by US regulations, and the ships were sold to Cunard. The *Adventurer* and *Ambassador* were smaller than *QE2* and were designed solely for cruising. They were operated under the name of Cunard Cruise Ships Ltd.

Two new cruise ships were added to the fleet in 1976, *Cunard Countess* and *Cunard Conquest.* The former was based in the Caribbean, and the latter, renamed *Cunard Princess* in 1977, sailed from San Juan in Puerto Rico. *Cunard Ambassador* caught fire on 13 September 1974 while en route to New Orleans to pick up cruise passengers. Her crew were taken off by the tanker *Tallulah.* After assessment of damage it was decided that it was impractical to rebuild her, so she was sold as a livestock carrier and renamed *Linda Clausen.* Her twin, *Cunard Adventurer* was sold in 1977 to Lauritz Kloster and renamed *Sunward II.*

On *QE2*'s arrival back from her maiden round-the-world cruise in 1974, it was announced that the CGT liner *France* was to be withdrawn from service. She was *QE2*'s main competition on the North Atlantic and her withdrawal allowed *QE2* to undertake more transatlantic sailings profitably.

In September 1976, the Trafalgar House chairman, Nigel Broackes, announced the purchase of twelve ships. These had been part of the Maritime Fruit Carriers fleet, which were chartered to the Salen Group. The Salen Group cancelled the contract and the Fruit Carrier business folded. The new additions to the Cunard fleet had traditional Cunard names ending in -ia: *Andania* (IV), *Servia* (III), *Carmania* (III), etc. Ten of these ships were re-chartered to Salen, and then to United Brands of America Inc. As Cunard reduced its non-passenger interests, the ships were sold off one by one.

In 1976, Trafalgar House owned the following shipping companies: Cunard, Atlantic Container Lines (ACL), ACL (Australia), Brocklebank, Port Line, Moss Tankers, Cunard-Brocklebank Bulkers, Fruit Carriers and Offshore Marine.

Above: Cunard Countess arrived the same year. Both ships spent much of their time cruising the Caribbean.

Above left: In 1976 *Cunard Conquest* was built. In 1977 she was renamed *Cunard Princess.*

Below left: Aimed squarely at the American market, the home port of the ships was San Juan, Puerto Rico.

Over the years, Cunard has come to the aid of the British Government when it required a merchant fleet during wartime. Indeed, this had been the reason that Cunard received subsidies for building vessels such as *Mauretania* and *Lusitania*. One of the Articles of Association of Cunard White Star was that the company should remain British. So, when the British dependency of the Falkland Islands was invaded by the Argentinean army on 2 April 1982, the British Government asked many of the major British shipping lines to lend their assistance. A British task force was requisitioned and five Cunard ships called up for active service. These were *Saxonia* (IV), *Atlantic Conveyor*, *Luminetta*, *Cunard Countess,* and, most surprisingly, *Queen Elizabeth 2*. QE2 and P&O's *Canberra* were used as troop carriers, as they were the largest and fastest ships in the British merchant fleet. The only Cunard war loss, *Atlantic Conveyor*, was destroyed when an Exocet missile hit her. After the war ended, another ship was ordered to replace her and she was called *Atlantic Conveyor* (II).

In May 1983, Trafalgar House acquired Norwegian American Cruise Lines. Although the Norwegian company was only four years old, it had acquired an enviable reputation amongst American cruisers as one of the best up-market cruise lines. Their ships *Sagafjord* and *Vistafjord* were amongst the most spacious and best run ships afloat. After the takeover, they retained their Norwegian crews and their lovely hull colours, only adding Cunard's orange-red and black-tipped funnels. The

Above: In 1976 Cunard acquired a fleet of ten cargo ships including *Alsatia*.

Left: Sagafjord and Vistafjord were acquired from the Norwegian American Line and proved to be a popular duo in the Cunard cruising fleet. Both ships retained light grey hulls but had their funnels painted in Cunard colours.

acquisition of the two ships gave Cunard the ability to expand their fleet, without the expense of building new ships.

Trafalgar House acquired a 5 per cent share in P&O in May 1983 and a subsequent takeover bid was referred to the Monopolies & Mergers Commission. Trafalgar House decided not to proceeed with the proposed merger.

The next additions to the fleet, *Sea Goddess I* and *Sea Goddess II*, were built for Norske Cruises. These ships took cruising to a new dimension. They were built for the elite cruise market. Each ship could carry just over 100 passengers and they were the most luxurious ships afloat. The ships were designed to be more like private yachts than cruise ships

Above left: Sagafjord was sold off to Saga Cruises and became *Saga Rose*. Her sister, shown here, remained in the Cunard fleet, albeit renamed as *Caronia*, until October 2004. In early 2005 she rejoins her sister, becoming *Saga Ruby*.

Above right: In 1982 the ferry MV *England* was acquired from DFDS and converted for cruising. She left the fleet in 1986 and went to Jeddah to be used as an accommodation ship.

Below left: Cunard also acquired Seabourn in 1986, along with its yacht-like small cruise ships, *Sea Goddess I* and *II*.

Below right: The the two *Sea Goddess* ships together.

Above: For a time in the early 1980s, *QE2* was painted in a grey colour scheme – which was discontinued after only one season, and one can see why.

Below: *QE2* was requisitioned for the Falklands War as a troopship, following her two older sisters and going to war. She returned to a hero's welcome in Southampton at the end of the conflict with 700 survivors of the *Coventry*, *Antelope* and *Ardent*.

and, being so small, were able to go into ports in which larger cruise ships were unable to berth. Unfortunately, due to social and economic factors, like the murder of an American on the *Achille Lauro* by terrorists and the American bombing raids on Libya, the elite American clientele at which the ships were marketed were deterred from crossing the Atlantic. The *Goddesses'* builder, Wartsilia, repossessed them, with the London commercial banks taking over the debt. Cunard then leased them on a twelve-year charter.

The winter of 1986 saw *QE2* in Bremerhaven for a £100 million refit. While in the dry dock, she was converted to diesel-electric drive, losing her steam turbines. The refit lasted 179 days and her cabins and interiors were extensively reworked. It was calculated that she had travelled further on her old steam turbines than both the *Queen Mary* and *Queen Elizabeth* together. For a relatively old ship £100 million was a lot of money to spend, but at the time it was calculated that a new ship of similar design would cost almost three times as much to build.

The Cunard Ellerman company was formed when Trafalgar House acquired Ellerman lines in 1987. Trafalgar House merged the company with their existing Cunard cargo division to create a new company. The new company gave Trafalgar House interests in more than one line as Ellerman also had shareholdings in other companies around the world. In addition to this, Cunard Ellerman also controlled Cunard Air Cargo, Moss Tankers and agencies in Portugal and Sweden, to name but a few subsidiaries.

The 1990 cruising fleet consisted of *QE2*, *Sagafjord*, *Vistafjord*, *Cunard Countess*, *Cunard Princess* and *Sea Goddess 1* and *2*.

In March 1996, Trafalgar House was sold to Kvaerner which was well known for its shipbuilding, engineering and construction companies. For Cunard, this meant that for the first time in its history it was to be wholly owned by a foreign company.

During its ownership, Kvaerner reduced Cunard's cruising fleet. The only ships to remain were *QE2* and *Vistafjord*. *Vistafjord* was renamed *Caronia* and provided a complementary service to *QE2*. However, *Sagafjord* – her sister ship – was chartered to TransOcean Cruises and they opereated her under the name *Gripsholm*. When this charter came to an end in 1997, *Sagafjord* was sold to Saga Holidays, and then renamed *Saga Rose*.

The other two sisters in the fleet, *Cunard Princess* and *Cunard Countess*, were sold. *Cunard Princess* went to the Mediterranean Shipping Company in 1995 and was renamed *Rhapsody*. Meanwhile, *Cunard Countess* was sold to Awani Cruises.

In May 1998, Kvaerner sold Cunard to the Carnival Corporation, which was expanding rapidly to become the largest cruise ship owner in the world. At the time of the sale, Cunard's fleet consisted of *QE2* and *Vistafjord*.

Chapter Six

From Strength to Strength

LE QUEEN MARY 2 à CHERBOURG-OCTEVILLE de 8 H à 23 H

Carnival's purchase of the Cunard line from Kvaerner proved to be the turnaround in Cunard's fortunes that the company needed. Cunard now had the backing of a major cruise company, that understood the market and had ships operating in almost every segment of it.

Carnival started in 1972, when it bought the Canadian Pacific liner *Empress of Canada* and transformed her into *Mardi Gras*. The company started offering 'fun cruises' for middle-class Americans. Prior to this, there was a widespread belief that cruising was both expensive and that it was for 'geriatrics and their parents'. Carnival reinvented the market and began offering cheap cruises for Americans who were determined to enjoy their vacation time.

In 1975, *Mardi Gras* was joined by *Carnivale*, the former *Empress of Britain*, and then in 1978 by the former *SA Vaal*, which was renamed *Festivale*. *Tropicale* was Carnival's first new-build cruise ship in 1982. Offering exactly what its customers demanded, Carnival went from strength to strength and now owns over nineteen cruise ships in its own right and has acquired many other brands such as Holland America, Seabourn, Windstar and, more recently, P&O/Princess.

Carnival's acquisition of Cunard in 1998 allowed Carnival to have a foothold in the luxury end of the cruising market. Carnival decided to keep the distinctive branding of Cunard, and added a few of its own touches. The price Carnival paid for Cunard reflected as much the value of the brand as it did the value of the company as a whole.

In the early 1990s Trafalgar House had planned a new transatlantic liner codenamed Q5. This never progressed beyond the drawing board. Carnival wanted

Previous page: At Guernsey on her maiden call in April 2004, *Queen Mary 2* is a majestic sight.

Left and opposite: Into the new millennium; it was announced that a new Cunard liner was to be built. To be named *Queen Mary 2*, she was to be the largest passenger ship in the world, tipping the scales at 150,000grt and being about 100ft longer than any other passenger ship built. Designed to cope with the rigours of the North Atlantic, she is a true ocean liner.

to build on *QE2*'s success. The *Queen Elizabeth 2* always had a reputation of being a 'luxury' cruise ship, but the new 'luxury' cruising market was overtaking her. For the Carnival accountants, *Caronia* was not large enough for the company to enjoy large profits from her. Both she and *QE2* were getting older and, although paid for, were not as profitable as larger ships with more passengers and smaller crews.

The 'Queen' name had always been associated with Britishness and quality, and it was important that any new Cunard liner had the 'Queen' name attached to it. The *Queen Mary* and *Queen Elizabeth* were amongst the most famous ocean liners in the world. They were instantly recognisable and very well known and loved on both sides of the pond.

Design work started on a new superliner, the first ocean liner to be built since *QE2* in 1969. Carnival announced the building of its new liner *Queen Mary 2* (Q6) in June 1998. She was to break with tradition and be the first Cunarder built at the Chantiers de L'Atlantique shipyard in France. Entering service in January 2004, at 150,000 tons, she is the largest ocean liner ever built and 113ft longer than the original *Queen Mary*. Her maiden voyage from Southampton to Fort Lauderdale took place on 11 January 2004.

Like her predecessors, *Queen Mary 2* has a multitude of 'firsts' to her name. She is the first ocean liner built at over 150,000 tons, and she is the first to have a planetarium. She has the latest navigation and propulsion systems, and the most modern interiors. Indeed, since the demise of Concorde, she is now the only way to arrive in New York in style. Her 2005 season has twenty-six transatlantic crossings, more than any Cunard ship has made since 1983. In 2004 *Caronia* left the fleet to rejoin her older sister with Saga Cruises.

On 14 December 2001, the Carnival Corporation announced that it had signed the contract with the Fincantieri shipyard in Italy to build another new Cunard ship. The new ship, to be called *Queen Victoria*, was to be 85,000 tons, carrying almost 2,000 passengers. In a corporate fleet shuffle, this ship has gone to P&O to become *Arcadia* with a new *Queen Victoria* being built in a more traditional liner style to enter service in 2007.

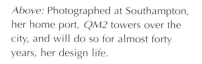

Above: Photographed at Southampton, her home port, *QM2* towers over the city, and will do so for almost forty years, her design life.

Far right: Built in 1969, *QE2* has but a few years left in service. She has become one of the icons of Scottish industrial might and is shown here next to another on her 2001 visit to South Queensferry, Scotland.

Right: A bust of Queen Mary in the Queens Room of *Queen Mary 2*.

The Cunard name will live on through these new ships, each with a design life of forty years. They will carry on the Cunard tradition of 'safety first, then excellent service' long after *QE2* has been withdrawn from service. At almost forty, she has little time left, but the new Queens are destined to keep the Cunard name alive for another two generations.

In its 165-year history, Cunard has become synonymous with ocean liner travel and it seems fitting that its modern-day fleet carries on the traditions that Samuel Cunard himself established in 1840. Although his company is no longer British, its very Britishness is what has secured its future within the Carnival organisation. May Cunard have another 165 years of history for future historians to write about.